Coy Candour

By M Renae Dubois

Contents

Introduction

This is the third of a series of semi-biographical verse-novels which explore head injury and its effects on the psyche; sex-work from a positive lived experience; relationships; and identity. My academic and aesthetic instincts have always been guided by an interest in philosophy, specifically logic, as well as ethics. I'm also drawn to language, including etymology and semantics.

Part One

Profession Obsession

Sex work, a Profession
It directly leaves impressions
To do, to say, to think, to be
To them an indiscretion

They think we do the same things
As each and one another
But cower in confusion when we
Insist they use a rubber

Like that is something unusual
Something ill defined
You're dreaming mate, your culture is
Coarse and unrefined

They think we all have long hair
Big Boobs and Pleaser heels
They think we all have boyfriends
Who cheat and from us steal

What they think would say a lot
If they were honest in their head
But they don't even acknowledge
That it's just what they have read

Amongst their friends they're oh so tough
That image falls away
When the door is opened and now, they're here
Of course they want to play

Uncontrive

Quite a living you are having
You don't take things in half shots!
Looking quizzically, I asked him,
D'ya mean like vodka on the rocks?
Perplexed, then breaks out laughing
His friend is not impressed
But he's not likely to be, anyway
As I often wear a dress
Artless, he accused, and would
Not look me in the eye
I felt the condescension hit me
Like arrows on the fly
I stumbled homeward somehow
But I felt that I'd been seen
But I didn't know of what he saw
Or what artless seemed to mean
A doubt it germinated in
My soul but it came with
An acknowledgement of artistry

In ignorant type bliss

Began begotten

I don't think I knew what the danger was
I don't think that I even cared
I went out, to get some of what, all of
My friends they had already shared

So, my partners were all of these old guys
Who wouldn't go taking me home
After playing the game somewhat badly
They'd force me to get home alone

They left me when they were deflated
Their energy was totally spent
So, tomorrow I'd see my big gay friend
And sit around getting full bent

Convinced to choose prostitution
Like a choice that would make some more sense
To fire my ethical metal
Though young, I developed the rest

Intent

Many are pleasant, many are kind

They usually show up if they're going to, on time

Their intentions are simple

They don't want for much

Just someone to talk to and

Someone to touch

It isn't important to mess with their heads

Cos they're not complicated,

Not when its sex

They all have unique ways

To be satisfied

Cos, they know that in our time,

There's no need to lie

I like these guys, most of them

In their own way

They share vulnerability

Although they do pay

It's a tight rope we're walking

Not touching the floor

The reality, the basics

Of just wanting more

Motherfucking Me

My boyfriend has a problem with the things I do to earn
I do not listen to him anyway, cos I have cash to burn
He doesn't make as much or nearly half of what I do
And he bitches about the pain he's in, to his misogynistic
crew
The pain he's ins debatable cos I treat him fucking well
The things I do for him and his are all a fucking tell
They speak the truth of how kind I am, and the things
that matter most
Cos I give him so much better than the guys I fucking
host
He can keep his bellyaching for his therapist and leave
The business of making money to motherfucking me.

Sketch

The image of a form of you
A gesture or a look
I just don't want to put all of
Your personality in my book
'Tis enough I draw a sketch of you
An image represents
The kind of role you play
And what your deeds have meant
I don't carry a burning flame
I know they do get smothered
The expectations, perceived roles
Of always one another
Fatiguing, it is tiring
I can only take so much
So I keep it on the physical
And its only flesh you touch

Divine, Consign

Cool air, it hits her temple, as
She walks through sliding doors
She's walking out her tension
Shopping, her first amour

The lighting in the store befits
A luxury pantomime
The ladies feeling wicked for
Seeking out a style divine

Her hand rests on her belly
As she contemplates and looks
Should she focus on the fashion,
Or buy lots of lovely books?

She steps a little further in,
In the past, she would be helped
Nowadays the young assistants
Do not care for health nor wealth

She decides against conversing
She quickly walks away
From these shitheads with their mobiles
And all the games they play

They see her as she's leaving
And tossing back her hair
Her demeanour may be fleeting
But it causes them to stare

Part Two

Dignity

The worst part of working
At this job to date
Is the look on people's faces
When they see I'm overweight

A plain and cuddly girl like me
You wouldn't think could do it
You might even make presumptions
That I'll people-please, then rue it

It is, to me, important
To believe in something true
Not the vision that I saw
Or how it affected you

I had to have a certain faith
In my inherent worth
Find something real about me
That for once I do not curse

I'm glad I walked the lonely path

Of decisions, some regrets

I would gladly do it over

If I didn't have a bed

My self-esteem is not for sale

Regardless of my job

I still get the sullen looks, but

My dignity they can't rob

Turn

I wish I had the ability
To write like I could work

To simply make a decision
Place an ad and learn to twerk

I miss the wicked pleasures
Of setting up a space

Writing a catchy intro
Doing up my pretty face

Waiting for the clients
Who want to know my rates

Even though all of the details
Are on my own ad space

Then I get a good one

He's done this all before

Texts an introduction
And doesn't ask for more

The industry's so easy
It's so quick to make a buck

If I want to be a writer
I'll need a lot of luck

Intrepid

Allow me to ejaculate
With this raw word I'll escalate
The opinions that I hold inside
That do concern, definitely divide

I do not think that I was born
To work a living, like some sheep shorn
I'm lucky that I have a way
To fill my time, to work the day

In art and study, I am there
The feeling of success, Beware!
I passed one subject, now do two
I'm going to do a Bachelor's too

I wanted this from childhood since
I'm going to of my life to rinse
The people who would cause me shame
I will not talk to them again

I will deter their petty flow

Their bodies spent can now just go

Pleasure and Pain

Have you ever felt a pleasure
That was intense, like of a pain?
A sudden stimulation
That you went back for, and again
You feel the magic bullet
Like metal, it's a core
Of the part that is erected
That when touched, it feels so sore
The clients, when they reach me
Get me in this way
I cry out in simulation
Of pleasure, cos they pay
But it feels they're going too far
It feels like an assault
I have to take control here
Their energies to halt
I didn't come into this room
To be manhandled and abused
From now this client's number

Is blocked, his jobs refused

Moyster

The pearl of hidden wisdom
In the deep blue sea, a shell
There's a creature in there somewhere
But doesn't like being held

She grows the orb within her
While the flesh inside her swells
Her style is a refined one
But men know not what she held

They want the inner wisdom
But they know not of the pearl
They think the truth that's spoke of
Is in the warm flesh that unfurls

So, the pearl of wisdom's hidden
Until the right one comes along
Who knows how to shuck the oyster
And how to sing the song

Tool

The penis is a tool
That's horribly designed
The owner of it wants it to
Be ready all the time

But it's not, or it is fickle
Very temperamental
One hard minute it's all let's go
And the next? No elemental

He swats it and manhandles
He tries to flog it up
But the girl that's lying next to him
Is getting too fed up

The mood is gone and is replaced
By desperate male shame
Attempting bravado he will try,
But cannot play the game

Part Three

Bolt

I've learned that I cannot depend
On others for my care
I have to walk this life alone
Forever if I dare

It would be nice to have a friend
Someone to walk with
But I do not know where these strange folk
Work, associate, love, or live

I write a poem, read a book
Take a chance and have a look
But I do not know the rules out here
I'll make mistakes, of that I fear

I cannot be a laughingstock
I cannot leave this house unlocked
I want to leave, I want to live
I want to, of this heart, to give

I'd like to love a cherished friend
I will adapt, my will, will bend
Do you have what I might need?
A friendship grown, potential seed?

Please just try to give a fuck
I have only my bitter luck
That saw me withdraw into those
Suburbs anon, the neutral clothes

I want to live, break free and be
A vivid type of personality
I wish I could appeal some more
I wish I knew what it was for

Why do I exist at all?

Care

The fabric tears not gently
The seams will pull away
Costume of a character
Of a previous long day

Sheer cloth that did not nearly hide
The form that lay beneath
The flesh confessed a pressing need
Now relies on self-belief

To turn to other textures
Be elegant, demure
To not reveal the flesh but seek
Clothing that will cure

Crafting her own image
Styling the right tone
Wrapped within an aura
A warmth like from one's home

Bravado

The people who are scared of this
We do not notice, do not miss
They exist in another realm
The things we do would overwhelm
Notice how I think of me
Whenever I refer to we
It is my perspective here to take
What others feel for my own sake
I'm probably wrong but they are too
Your view belongs to only you

Swells and Dips

The ethics and integrity
Attempts to still the ship

To guide a path through storms and all
The currents and the rips

My ego and identity
Separate though conjoined

Work together to then weather, and
Not to let storms then destroy

We must form a set of boundaries
We will build some solid walls

Not let the bastards steal from us
And leave us both appalled

We have only this wooden boat

With place for each one who

Wants to search perimeters
Wants to live and do

The sharks of doubts surrounding
This boat upon the waves

Will not be feared or dwelt upon
Because our resolution stays

We begin our future here on top
Of very little known

The ocean deep will pull at us
Make us want to turn back home

There is no home; it's gone now, said
The captain at the wheel

The quiet determined character
In this metaphorical spiel

The captain is the stubborn will
He will not turn the ship

He'll continue on, and lead us to
A preferable friendship

Niece 1:

Living is a state of mind
An attitude you take

Knowing you can do it all
Just for its own sake

There is no one controlling you
If you just let it go

Discard the expectations
And go on with a flow

The things that hold you back are just
The things you bring around

The people who you love will need
To let you stand your ground

Maybe it's a sudden shift

Maybe much more slow

In order to create something
That you'll be proud to show
I wish for you the luck you need
But the courage that I speak

Is perhaps a little misguided
Cos it can get very bleak

I urge you to consider
Not to do it like I did

Maybe while you work on it
You should keep it under lid

In any case, you have the choice
To take it in the hand

Be a major player and
Make a bold, defiant stand

Part Four

Academic Aspiration

I'd really like to study
Delve into the past
I want to know who thought of it
And how long did it last
I want to examine relationships
People from before
How they went about
Expressing their amour
I'll have to learn of battles
That's all part of it
The women who may inspire the fight
And the men who do conflict
The fashion of the times will tell
More of trade and tribute
The designers and the merchants
Who bring it and contribute
I'm interested in the writing
What has come before,
The parchment tells us one view

Archaeology says much more
I just need to get a picture
A firm and real hold
Of the community that I live in
Within which I try to mould
A more realistic perspective
Of what is expected of me
And then I can find comfort
In acting uniquely

Rose vs Prose

Why is that the poem
That says love's like a rose
Is better in describing feeling
Than how the fresh daisy grows?

Maybe that's opinion
I certainly don't agree
I feel much more peace and joy
When my hands are clean and free

The rose and love that is referred
Is said to be quite deep
But why is it just the reality of
The investment that's so steep?

When I think of love and lovers
And it's likened to a rose
Then I am drawn to see the thorn
And the pain that with it goes

Is it deeper to be unhappy?

Is it superficial to be glad?

To feel the sunshine on you

And know you've not been had?

It's harder to be happy

And for that I think it's worth,

The title of profundity

In the poetry and verse

Time Rhyme

I'm touching on the deficits
Struggle all the time
The words are there but twisted
They don't want to hear my rhyme

They're teaching things I've heard of
Things I ought to know
But it's not what I am needing
It's not helping with the flow

I want to study literature
I really want to explore
Why these pages move me
Why I look for more

I'd like to study everything
Learn in my own way
But it doesn't work just like that
Uni teaches and I pay

Some of my opinions
I realise are for nought
They will not help achieve
The vision that I sought

So I'm finding it confronting
I'm finding it way too hard
Maybe I'll go back to being
An uneducated bard.

Playbook

Did you ever have a feeling?

Did you know you were going to write

a book?, or did it come to you

On a dark and stormy night?

I knew I was artistic, but I felt my art was shit

I knew I had to live, to create meaning out of this

Perhaps it was philosophy

That I was more drawn to

The exciting stretching tentacles

Of minds eyes, what they view

I actually knew I'd be alright and come into some cash

And this was couple of years before I had my head on

crash

I thought I'd be the lover or have lovers of my own

Spilling out from every corner of the world in which I

roam

But no, I didn't feel I knew what I really wanted to say

I just hoped for an exciting life, and my own philosophy

to play

Lit

Every decade gets better
The older I go
The more I am capable
The more that I know

I wouldn't have wanted
To miss out on youth
But I'm glad that it's over
And I'm now long in the tooth

The adventures I undertook
Kept me insane
I really would not want
To go through it again

I've burned in the fire
But now I arise
A poet, a phoenix
Flame lit up inside

Fatigue Float

The world, it isn't talking
It is feeling somewhat black
The visions are not coming
I'm feeling kind of slack

To inspire and prick the senses
To get back to what I know
To express disinhibition
To write with a sure flow

The ideas, they are not lining up
I don't always feel inspired
In the morning after concert
I am feeling somewhat tired

Not in limbs but in thought patterns
I was glowing from my talk
I do not always know the lesson
That I am being taught

It's a lifestyle of a poet
An artistic reverie
Of being home and feeling, waiting,
For a prompt that can then be

A poem or reflection
A wisdom there beheld
That I didn't know I knew of
And now it's out and spelled

The mysterious reception
When I read what I have wrote
Oh, I want it ever-present
I want to always float

a, b, c

a

What do I do with the guilt that I feel so?

Where do I lay down the load?

The cross that I carry is personal

With my conscience I walk memory's road

I wish I could go back and change some things

I'm seeking a salve for my sins

The knowledge of things that I did then

And those that I did offend

Perhaps in the honest reflection

I will finally come to a peace

When agonising my faults I am done with

When in a future, I can believe

b

But really, will it ever be over?

The worry, the stress, and the pain

The transgressions and errors I fall into

Behaviour that seems always the same

I cannot escape from this person,

Her instincts and character flaws

I am beholden to her apprehensions

But also her mission at core

To rely on a vision of pleasure

To construct one's own virtue ideal

Not to wallow in tempting depression

But to find something inside that's more real

Who could hope for a better solution

Than to find it was worth all the pain

And the joy that I feel is encompassing

Will hit no one quite like me the same

c

I hope that in things that I write here
That I'm finally making a point
I hope to give you some hope though
That its worth more than stories and joints
You are creating a past for yourself now
So find something to look back and say
Yeah I really enjoyed my time doing that
Even though I didn't earn any pay
Because life is here for the taking
And you don't have to be happy and glad
But you also can read a good book now
Even though you may feel somewhat sad
I encourage you to think it over
To give living aloud a good go
Cos the time it will move even swifter
And it's gone before you even know.

Part Five

2025

We do not know if we can say
The things that ought be said
We cannot post online the things
We think in our own head

The cameras are watching
The microphone is on
The things we think appear on our
Social media on their own

Everybody's lonely
But no one wants to say
That it's ok to come on over
That, yes, they want to play

The anxiety is palpable
And mixed with depths of rage
The older that I get I see
It's not just up to age

The people who are in power
They watch all this and dare,
The people, us! to question them
We wonder if they care

They set the tone, they mark the price
That we all have to pay
And if someone ends up locked in jail
There's not much we can say

Age

Figures that don't tell the truth

Their faces are a lie

The images they emulate

Are sometimes very dire

The palette displays many sorts

Of textures and of tones

But it is just a coloured wash

Over decaying bones

They're dying, getting older

They're not meaning what they say

They're just trying to get through this

Ere their eternal beds to lay

Reality

Reality, it does not exist
Except in minds that experience this
The thoughts, impressions, and the hate
Determine partly of our fate
What we think begins anew
What they think it's not of you
They're thinking of themselves at first
But do not wish on you the worst
They do not care, they think they do
Remember now, it's up to you

Layers

Like the layers of an onion
The search for inner core
The layers of perception peeled
But intact they tell much more
The skin that is discarded
In the therapeutic way
Rips apart the girl's impressions
Disregarding what will stay
The juicy flesh that makes up part
Of her views which are beheld
Her selective inner vision
The juicy tales it tells
To seek an inner core seems like
Where the truth will lie
But it's in layers of perception
That define the days gone by

Weight of Fate

The quiet administration that goes on behind closed
doors
No one wants to let them know the whys and the
wherefores
My poetry it sings at times, its deceptively divine
But when I go to put together the story, to refine
I am burdened by the weight of the dire capacity
Of my strength but all the weaknesses, the harsh reality
The truth must be created, I must choose a story in
The examples in the rhythm of the living in the sin
Its exciting, overwhelming, I can be whoever I want
The poems though reality, are manipulated and a front
A story that is memoir will always slant the tale
And I guess that I am as guilty of the flex and the regale
It's just weird I take reality, and raw emotional weight
And create a different history and an alternative future
fate.

Integrity

The answers to your questions
You have to find within
The truth is for the seeking
And first you must begin
Take a different attitude
To the things that they propose
Choose the most appropriate thing
Before resentment grows
They want you to abide by
The conventions that are in place
But you've got to be at one with
What you see in your own face
You've got to find a niche or nook
In which to invest time
Passion too and discipline
So your creations do align
Examine your own morals
From whence did they arrive?
Are you sure that they are what you need
To make your bright light shine?

You do not have to be the same

As everyone before

You do not have to feel a guilt,

Or shame, you can ignore

Be your own creation

Style your health yourself

Embrace the inner anxiety

Say it how you felt

Be true, build an integrity

Always pay back debts

Build a personality

That no one can upset

Souls Afloat

They're floating through the atmosphere
But coming through her veins
They're here to feel the music
Cos the magic does remain

She opens up her mind and lets
The past in her ferment
And the people who live through her
Can embrace and not lament

They see through her physicality
They experience the now
They're amazed at all the women
Wearing pants, machines that plough

The screens remain a mystery
Will not to them make sense
But the music and the visions are
Both full and most intense

They welcome the conduit for
Them, spirits in the air
They appreciate the visions of
The fashions and the flair

She'll stay in this flow moment,
And perhaps will never leave
She is the raw transmittance
And through her, they can breathe

Part Six

Chappy

Cheerily he chuckles
And pulls on a long lobe
His eyes they are a-twinkling
As he sees his wife disrobe
He never really grew up,
Although his nose grew large
He's balding and gone grey now
His muscles are not hard
But he loves his wife and cherishes
The time she spends to flirt
With an old dog like her husband
Who just loves a bit of skirt

Violet Light

Violet cascading
Streaming down from the sky
The beauty and majesty
Of all up on high

How could you fail
To believe in a god
Who would give us this vision
The trees and the wood

But it's not only vision
That encapsulates time
The sound of the birds and
The musical rhyme

Sensations of walking
Bare foot in the grass
The droplets of dew
The wind while it passed

It lifts up goose pimples
On my bare arms
My scalp it is tickling
This moment will last

Thank God for this image
The sounds and the touch
I'm feeling exhilarated
I'm feeling His love

The End

They die, they do not want to
Their oxygen is cut off
Their voices suffocated
Squeeze out their final cough
No longer to endure the pain
No longer strapped in beds
While deathly howls fill the ward
Crying out in their distress
The home for these old gentlefolk
Is theirs unto the end
Most of them don't even know
How it all began
Horrifying morbidity
Stink, decay and death
The mortifying reality
Of end of life, last breath

Sanctuary

The house it stood there proudly
While the wind whipped up the leaves
The autumnal shades are speaking
Of weather's tiredness, how she grieves
The shingles on the roof appear
To be a part of rusted vision
A fatigue and a weariness
The need to make decisions
The weathered beams that make up all
The walls and verandas round
Are painted in a conducive shade
An orange sort of brown
This countryside is beautiful
Especially days like these
While autumn sun is setting
And there's a slightly chiller breeze

Oh No, an Emo!

Oh God you must be kidding!
An emo! Tell me no
I can't believe you're with him!
He has piercings in his nose
Violet hair, excited
But his mood is much repressed
He writes verse but it is maudlin
And he wears a dress!
Do you loan him all your lipstick?
Does he share your eye make-up?
Dear Lord, I can't get over
How my daughter has fucked up
With a punk! 'No, he's an emo'
Does it even really matter?
Daughter, listen when I tell you
That he's going to get fatter
In his older years he'll grow out of
The style you think is cool
And he'll try to be still relevant

When really, he's a tool

An End

Eluding her eyes, averting
Looking to the side
He watches as the raindrops
Fall from the umbrella, glide

Looking down in guilt he sees
Her feet are clad in boots
Standing in a puddle
He doesn't think; he seems aloof

He wants to turn his back on her
Turn and walk away
But he can feel her eyes upon him
And he knows he's not OK

Putting one hand in his pants
Eager for distraction
He finds a ticket in his pocket
And thinks of taking action

He braves himself to look at her
To gauge what she is thinking
He sees that she's still holding hope
And dismayed his mood starts sinking

I got to go, he mumbles
And she raises an eyebrow
I guess I'll see you next time
That's if you'll allow

She doesn't answer and he turns
And walks quickly away
He doesn't want her to see his tears
Or the pain he tries to allay

She watches him get smaller
And in her mind, she thinks
It's sad to see him angry
But worse when his mood sinks

Sighing, she will gather

Her thoughts and actions to
Get home and out of this rain
This relationship she will rue

Ten To Go

10 the eyes narrow

9 they see the clock

8 he grabs the handles

7 chassis rock

6 he breathes in deeply

5 a strong exhale

4 sounds are forgotten

3 foot on the rail

2 he revs the engine

1 it's now or not

Green the light is go now

Fuck this engine's hot

Psychosis.

I'm kicking goals, I'm hitting targets, I'm surpassing
KPIs.
I have started to market product and I have my inner
drive
If it were only that these bureaucrats
Would just stop and read their mail
Then I could just halt a half a minute and be able to
exhale
They're not answering must try harder
Must not let the company down
Must work hard to fill this hollow
From the business district now
Here we go now, must be spam, no that looks
Like official letterhead
But it couldn't be that really
It's got to be in my own head
What you doing, an assessment?
Well, it couldn't be of me
I'm succeeding I'm triumphant I am full of tenacity

That's the problem Not a problem

Oh, you cannot be correct

I've been working at this desk

I have placed all of the bets

Gambler

I don't know what you want from me, you're confusing
me to bits
I think that your hypocrisy is giving me the shits

You say that you don't like it when I spend money on a
dress
But you take all of your income and place it on a bet

If you want me to be serious then we'll have to have a
talk
Coz I'm telling you my darling, I'm about to fuckin walk

I will not be a widow when my husband's still alive
And I won't be made dependant on the government to
survive

Not if I can help it, there's got to be a way
But first we need to set aside our meagre weekly pay

We can't afford to gamble, we can't afford to bet
We're not going to win the lotto, I'm not going to give
you head

Understand something my darling, you are a family man
And the rest of us are trying to stick to the basic plan

Of getting an education, of working for some cash
And bringing up our children to know how to build a
stash

Light

Stars prickle in the night sky
The spikes of fiery light
Claiming a growing shadow
Of the outback sky at night
Like a veil across the heavens
A fabric lightly wisps
Like a brush with loving gestures
And a solemn special kiss
Maybe it's a faery
A figure up above
Who comes with great intentions
To show me all the love
The universe it beckons
It tells me it's OK
I'm not going to get in trouble
There's no need to run away

Enfin

A stillness, a fulfilled-ness
To be steady in my head
To feel the peace the inner breeze
All the wisdom that I read
I can't betray the ones before
Cannot state what others meant
But I know that in my mission
There will be no one heaven sent
Thank the wind and all the sunshine
Regard the storms and mind the hail
I cannot live for others' reasons
That to me is beyond the pale
Towards a future I am travelling
And the truth's becomes my goal
I will seek it, I will find it
I am on a fucking roll!

www.ingramcontent.com/pod-product-compliance
Lightning Source LLC
Chambersburg PA
CBHW062114040426
42337CB00042B/2369